THE CLASSIFICATION OF EVERYTHING

The
Classification
of Everything

Melvil Dewey
John Mark Ockerbloom
Pinch Village LLC

The classification system presented in this volume is based largely on Dewey's *Decimal System* (1876) and Ockerbloom's *Free Decimal Correspondence* (2010). It has been updated for improved benefit to librarians. It shortens subject headings, provides a more intuitive sequence of topics, and reduces the number of classes to nine—freeing up the tenth class for any purpose of the librarian's choosing. It retains Dewey's classic preface and card catalog appendix, removes his outdated index, retains most of Ockerbloom's scope and nomenclature, and adds guidance for digital collections.

FIRST EDITION, APRIL 2015 © PINCH VILLAGE LLC

To learn to classify is in itself an education.

—*Alex Bain*

PREFACE

The plan of the following Classification was first developed early in 1873. It was the result of several months' study of library economy as found in some hundreds of books and pamphlets, and in over fifty personal visits to various American libraries. In this study, the author became convinced that the usefulness of these libraries might be greatly increased without additional expenditure. Three years practical use of the system here explained, leads him to believe that it will accomplish this result; for with its aid, the catalogues, shelf lists, indexes, and cross-references essential to this increased usefulness, can be made more economically than by any other method which he has been able to find. The system was devised for cataloguing and indexing purposes, but it was found on trial to be equally valuable for numbering and arranging books and pamphlets on the shelves.

The library is first divided into nine special libraries which are called Classes. These Classes are Philosophy, Religion, etc., and are numbered with the nine digits. Thus Class 9 is the Library of History; Class 6, the Library of Art; Class 3, the Library of Religion. These special libraries or Classes are then considered independently, and each one is separated again into nine special Divisions of the main subject. These Divisions are numbered from 1 to 9 as were the Classes. Thus 39 is the 9th Division (Physiology) of the 4th Class (Government). A final division is then made by separating each of these Divisions into nine Sections which are numbered in the same way, with the nine digits. Thus 323 is the 3rd Section (Geometry) of the 2nd Division (Mathematics) of the 4th Class (Government). This number, giving Class, Division, and Section, is called the Classification or Class Number, and is applied to every book or pamphlet belonging to the library. All the Geometries are thus numbered 323, all the Mineralogies 359, and so throughout the library, all the books on any given subject bear the number of that subject in the scheme. Where a 0 occurs in a class number, it has its normal zero power. Thus, a book numbered 320, is Class 4, Division 2, but *no* Section. This signifies that the book treats of the Division 320 (Mathematics) in general, and is not limited to any one Section, as is Geometry, marked 323. If marked 300, it would indicate a treatise on Mathematics in general, limited to *no* Division. A zero occurring in the first place would in the same way show that the book is limited to *no* Class. The classification is mainly made by subjects or content regardless of *form*; but it is found practically useful to make an additional distinction in these general treatises, according to the form of treatment adopted. Thus, in Engineering we have a large number of books treating of Engineering in general, and so having a 0 for the Division number. These books are then divided into Sections, as are those of the other Classes according to the form they have taken on. We have the Philosophy of technology, Formulas, Dictionaries, Essays, Periodicals, Societies, Education, Inventions, and History,—all having the common subject, ENGINEERING, but treating it in these varied forms. These form distinctions are introduced here because the number of general works is large, and the numerals allow of this division, without extra labor for the numbers from 501 to 509 would otherwise be unused. They apply *only* to the general treatises, which, without them, would have a class number ending with two zeros. A Dictionary of Medicine is 510, not 503, for every book is assigned to the *most specific head that will contain it,* so that 503 is limited to Dictionaries or Cyclopedias of Technology *in general.* In the same way a General Cyclopedia or Periodical treats of no one class, and so is assigned to the Class 0. These books treating of no special class, but general in their character, are divided into Cyclopedias, Periodicals, etc. No difficulty is found in following the arithmetical law and omitting the initial zero, so these numbers are printed 31, 32, etc., instead of 031, 032, etc.

The selection and arrangement of the thousand headings of the classification cannot be explained in detail for want of space. In all the work, philosophical theory and accuracy have been made to yield to practical usefulness. The impossibility of making a satisfactory classification of all knowledge as preserved in books, has been appreciated from the first, and nothing of the kind attempted. Theoretical harmony and exactness has been repeatedly sacrificed to the practical requirements of the library or to the convenience of the department in the college. As in every scheme, many minor subjects have been put under general heads to which they do not strictly belong. In some cases these headings have been printed in a distinctive type, e. g., 629 OLD ENGLISH, under ENGLISH LANGUAGE. The rule has been to assign these subjects to the most nearly allied heads, or where it was thought they would be most useful. The only alternative was to omit them altogether. If any such omission occurs, it is unintentional and will be supplied as soon as discovered. Wherever practicable the heads have been so arranged that each subject is preceded and followed by the most nearly allied subjects and thus the greatest convenience is secured both in the catalogues and on the shelves. Theoretically, the division of every subject into just nine heads is absurd. Practically, it is desirable that the classification be as minute as possible without the use of additional figures, and the decimal principle on which our scheme hinges allows nine divisions as readily as a less number. This principle has proved wholly satisfactory in practice though it appears to destroy proper co-ordination in some places. It has seemed best in our library to use uniformly three figures in the class number. This enables us to classify certain subjects very minutely, giving, for example, an entire section to Chess. But the History of England has only one section, as our scheme is developed, and thus the two might be said to be co-ordinated. The apparent difficulty in such cases is entirely obviated by the use of a fourth figure, giving nine sub-sections to any subject of sufficient importance to warrant closer classification. In history where the classification is made wholly by countries, additional figures are added to give divisions into *periods.* As the addition of each figure gives a ten-fold division, any desired degree of minuteness may be secured in the classing of special subjects. The apparent lack of co-ordination arises from the fact that only the first three figures of these more important heads are as yet printed, the fourth figure and the sub-sections being supplied on the catalogues in manuscript. Should the growth of any of these sub-sections warrant it, additional figures will be added, for the scheme admits of expansion without limit.

The arrangement of headings has been sometimes modified to secure a mnemonic aid in numbering and finding books without the Index. For instance, the scheme is so arranged that China has always the number 1. In Ancient History, it has the first section, 831: in Modern History, under Asia, it has 851: in Philology, the Chinese language appears as 695.1. After the same manner the Indian number is 2; Egyptian, 4; English, 2; German, 3; French, 4; Italian, 5; Spanish, 6; European, 4; Asian, 5; African, 6; North American, 7; South American, 8; and so for all the divisions by languages or countries. The Italian 5, for instance, will be noticed in 035, 055, 650, 805, and 845. This mnemonic principle is specially prominent in Philology and Literature and their divisions, and in the *form* distinctions used in the first 9 sections of each class. Materials, Methods, or Theory occurring anywhere as a head, bears always the number 1. Dictionaries and Cyclopedias, 3; Essays, 4; Periodicals, 5; Associations, Institutions, and Societies, 6; Education, 7; Collections, 9. In the numerous cases where several minor heads have been grouped together under the head Other, it always bears the number 9. Wherever practicable, this principle is carried out in sub-dividing the sections. For instance, the Geology of North America, which bears the number 367 is sub-divided by adding the *sections* of 870 (History of North America). The Geology of Mexico then bears the number 367.2: mnemonically, the first 4 is the Government number; the second 6, Geology; the 7, North America; and the 2, Mexico. Any library attendant or reader after using the scheme a short time will recognize at a glance, any catalogue or ledger entry, book or pamphlet, marked 367.2 as something on the Geology of Mexico. Users of the scheme will notice this mnemonic principle in several hundred places in the classification, and will find it of great practical utility in numbering and finding books without the aid of Catalogue or Index, and in determining the character of any book simply from its call number as recorded on the book, on all its catalogue and cross reference cards, on the ledger, and in the check box.

In naming the headings, brevity has been secured in many cases at the sacrifice of exactness. It was thought more important to have short, familiar titles for the headings than that the names given should express with fullness and exactness the character of all books catalogued under them. Many subjects, apparently omitted, will be found in an Index, assigned, with allied subjects, to a heading which bears the name of the most important only. Reference to this Subject Index will decide at once any doubtful points.

In arranging books in the classification, as in filling out the scheme, practical usefulness has been esteemed the most important thing. The effort has been to put each book under the subject to the student of which it would be most useful. The content or the real subject of which a book treats, and not the form or the accidental wording of the title, determines its place. Following this rule, a Philosophy of Art is put with Art, not with Philosophy; a History of Mathematics, with Mathematics, not with History; for the philosophy and history are simply the *form* which these books have taken. The true content or subject is Art, and Mathematics, and to the student of these subjects they are most useful. The predominant tendency or obvious purpose of the book, usually decides its class number at once; still many books treat of two or more different subjects, and in such cases it is assigned to the place where it will be most useful, and underneath the class number are written the numbers of any other subjects on which it also treats. These *Cross References* are given both on the plate and the subject card as well as on the cross reference card. If a book treats of a majority of the sections of any division, it is given the Division number instead of the most important Section number with cross references.

Collected works, libraries, etc., are either kept together and assigned like individual books to the most specific head that will contain them; or assigned to the most prominent of the various subjects on which they treat with cross references from the others; or are separated and the parts classed as independent works. Translations are classed with their originals.

The Alphabetical Subject Index is designed to guide, both in numbering and in finding the books. In numbering, the most specific head that will contain the book having been determined, reference to that head in the Index will give the class number to which it should be assigned. In finding books on any given subject, reference to the Index will give the number under which they are to be sought on the shelves, in the Shelf Catalogue, or in the Subject Catalogue. The Index gives after each subject the number of the class to which it is assigned. Most names of countries, towns, animals, plants, minerals, diseases, etc., have been omitted, the aim being to furnish an Index of Subjects on which books are written, and not a Gazetteer or a Dictionary of all the nouns in the language. Such subjects will be found as special chapters or sections of books on the subjects given in the Index. The names of individual subjects of biographies will be found in the Class List of Biography. Omissions of any of the more general subjects will be supplied when brought to notice.

In arranging the books on the shelves, the absolute location by shelf and book number is wholly abandoned, the relative location by class and book number being one of the most valuable features of the plan. The class number serves also as the location number and the shelf number in common use is entirely dispensed with. Accompanying the class number is the *book* number, which prevents confusion of different books on the same subject. Thus the first Geometry catalogued is marked 323-1; the second 323-2, and so on to any extent, the last number showing how many books the library has on that subject. The books of each section are all together, and arranged by book numbers, and these sections are also arranged in simple numerical order throughout the library. The call number 323-11 signifies not the 11th book on shelf 323; or alcove 4, range 2, shelf 3, as in most libraries, but signifies the 11th book in subject 323 or the 11th Geometry belonging to the library. In finding the book, the printed numbers on the backs are followed, the upper being the class and the lower the book number. The class is found in its numerical order among the classes as the shelf is found in the ordinary system: the book in its numerical order in the class. The shelves are not numbered, as the increase of different departments, the opening of new rooms, and any arrangement of classes to bring the books most circulated nearest to the delivery desk, will bring different class numbers on a given shelf. New books as received are numbered and put into place, in the same way that new titles are added to the card catalogue.

The single digit occasionally prefixed to the book number, e.g. the 3 in 421-3-7 is the nearest height in decimeters of books too large to be put on the regular library shelves, which are only 2-1/2 decimeters apart. The great mass of the library consists of 2-decimeter books, the size numbers of which are omitted. Books from 2-1/2 to 3-1/2 decimeters in height have 3 prefixed to the book number, and are found on the bottom shelf of each range. The larger sizes are prefixed with 4, 5, etc., and are found on the special shelves provided, in order to avoid the great waste of space otherwise occasioned by the relative location. By this use of the size numbers a close economy of space is secured.

Thus all the books on any given subject are found standing together, and no additions or changes ever separate them. Not only are all the books on the subject sought, found together, but the most nearly allied subjects precede and follow, they in turn being preceded and followed by other allied subjects as far as practicable. Readers not having access to the shelves find the short titles arranged in the same order on the Shelf Catalogue, and the full titles, imprints, cross references, notes, etc., on the Subject Catalogue. The uncatalogued pamphlets treating of any subject bear the same class number and are arranged on the shelves immediately after the books of each section.

In both the Authors' Catalogue and the Subject Index, brevity has been studied because of the economy, but more because of the much greater ease of reference to a short title catalogue. The custom of giving full titles, etc., under authors, and only references or very brief titles under subjects, has been reversed. A reader seeking a book of a *known author*, in the vast majority of cases, wants simply the number by which to call for it, and can find it much sooner in a brief title catalogue. In the rare cases where more is needed the class number refers instantly to all these facts on the cards. On the other hand, a reader seeking books on a *known subject*, needs the full title, imprint, cross-references, and notes, to enable him to choose the book best suited to his wants.

The Subject Catalogue is a full title Shelf List on cards and is for the use of the public. The Shelf List is a short title Subject Catalogue in book form, made of separate sheets laced into an Emerson binder, and is for official use. We thus have without extra labor, both full and short title Subject Catalogues and Shelf Lists. The public Authors' Catalogue is a printed volume; the official Authors' Catalogue or Index is on cards. As a result each of the public

Catalogues is checked by an official Catalogue; each of the card Catalogues by a book Catalogue; each of the brief title catalogues by a full title catalogue—an advantage that will be appreciated by all librarians desiring accuracy of administration and catalogues.

The Arabic numerals can be written and found more quickly, and with less danger of confusion or mistake, than any other symbols whatever. Therefore the Roman numerals, capitals and small letters, and similar symbols usually found in systems of classification are entirely discarded and by the exclusive use of Arabic numerals in their regular order throughout the shelves, classifications, indexes, catalogues and records, there is secured the greatest accuracy, economy, and convenience. This advantage is specially prominent in comparison with systems where the name of the author or the title must be written in calling for or charging books and in making references.

Throughout the catalogues the number of a book shows not only *where* it is but *what* it is. On the library accounts the character of each person's reading is clearly indicated by the numbers charged, and the minutest statistics of circulation in any subject are made by simply counting the call slips in the check box, and recording the number against the class number in the record.

By the use of size numbers the greatest possible economy of space may be secured, for the size distinction may be made for every inch or even less if desired, and this without additional labor, as it will be seen that the size figure, when introduced, requires one less figure in the book number, and so does not increase the number of digits as would at first appear.

Parts of sets, and books on the same or allied subjects, are never separated as they are sure to be, sooner or later, in every library arranged on the common plan, unless it be frequently re-arranged and re-catalogued. The great expense of this re-cataloguing makes it impracticable except for a few very wealthy libraries. In this system the catalogue and book numbers remain unchanged through all changes of shelving, buildings, or arrangement. In addition to its own peculiar merits, this plan has all the advantages of the card catalogue principle and of the relative location, which have been used and very strongly approved by prominent libraries.

As in the card catalogue system, there is room for indefinite expansion without devices or provisions. Space is the only requisite and if the shelf room is exhausted, the floor space is equally good, except for the inconvenience of stooping.

Some prominent opponents of classed catalogues have admitted that the Subject Index, in deciding where to class a book at first, and where to look for it ever afterwards, has removed their strongest objections. Certainly it would be impossible to make an Index more cheaply or more easy of reference, it being a single alphabet, of single words, followed by single numbers.

These class numbers applied to pamphlets have proved specially satisfactory. The number is written on the upper left corner and the pamphlets are arranged either in pamphlet cases with the books on the same subject or on special shelves divided every decimeter by perpendicular sections. As each pamphlet is examined when received into the library, it is the work of a single moment to pencil on it its class number. There is no expense whatever incurred, and yet the entire pamphlet resources of the library on any subject can be produced almost instantly. The immense advantages of this plan over those in common use, both in economy and usefulness, will be appreciated by every librarian caring for a pamphlet collection. A catalogue of authors may be made on slips if desired. The pamphlets themselves are the best Subject Catalogue.

Though designed wholly for library use, the plan has proved of great service in preserving newspaper clippings in large envelopes arranged by class numbers; and more especially in taking the place of the common note-book and Index Rerum. Slips of uniform size are used with the class number of the subject written on the corner. Minute alphabetical headings are used under each class number, the slips being arranged in numerical order like the Subject Card Catalogue. Clippings and notes arranged in this way are at all times their own complete index, and have the same advantages over the common scrap and note-books that the Subject Catalogue has over the Accessions Book, in looking up the resources of the library on any given subject. Those who have tried this method are so enthusiastic in its praise that it seemed worthy of mention in this place.

The plan was adopted in the Amherst College Library in 1873, and the work of transferring the entire library to the new catalogue at once commenced. It was found entirely practicable to make the change gradually, as means allowed, without interfering in any appreciable degree with the circulation of the books. The three years trial to which it has been there subjected has more than justified the claims of its friends, and it is now printed with the more confidence on this account. It has been kept in manuscript up to this time, in order that the many minor details might be subjected to actual trial and modified where improvement was possible. The labor involved in preparing the Classification and Index has been wholly beyond the appreciation of any who have never attempted a similar task. Much valuable aid has been rendered by specialists in many departments, and nearly every member of the Faculty has given advice from time to time. Among the many to whom thanks are due, special mention should be made of Mr. C.A. Cutter, the librarian of the Boston Athenæum, and Mr. John Fiske, of the Harvard University library, for valuable suggestions and appreciative criticism. While these friends are in no way responsible for any remaining imperfections in the scheme, they should have credit for many improvements which have been made during these three years of revision. The essential character of the plan has remained unchanged from the first. Doubtless other improvements are still possible, and it is hoped that users of the scheme will call attention to any proposed change in the naming or arrangement of the headings, or to any omission which should be supplied in the Subject Index.

Before printing, the plan was submitted to quite a number of librarians for criticism. Among the hundreds of points raised as to its practical workings and usefulness there was only one in which it was not shown to be equal or superior to any other system known. This objection applied only to the arrangement on the shelves; not at all to the catalogues or indexes. It was, that in this relative location, a book which this year stands, e.g., at the end of a certain shelf; may not be on that shelf at all another year, because of the uneven growth of the parts of the library. This slight objection inheres in any system where the books are arranged by *subjects* rather than by windows, doors, shelves, and similar non-intellectual distinctions.

In this hurriedly prepared account of his plan, the author has doubtless failed to meet many objections which may be raised and which he could easily answer. He would therefore ask the privilege of replying personally to any such objections, where they arise, believing that it will be possible to answer, if not all, at least a very large proportion.

In his varied reading, correspondence, and conversation on the subject, the author doubtless received suggestions and gained ideas which it is now impossible for him to acknowledge. Perhaps the most fruitful source of ideas was the *Nuovo Sistema di Catalogo Bibliografico Generale* of Natale Battezzati, of Milan. Certainly he is indebted to this system adopted by the Italian publishers in 1871, though he has copied nothing from it. The plan of the St. Louis Public School Library, and that of the Apprentices' Library of New York, which in some respects resemble his own, were not seen till all the essential features were decided upon, though not given to the public. In filling the nine classes of the scheme the inverted Baconian arrangement of the St. Louis Library has been followed. The author has no desire to claim original invention for any part of his system where another has been before him, and would most gladly make specific acknowledgment of every aid and suggestion were it in his power to do so. With these general explanations and acknowledgments he submits the scheme, hoping it may prove as useful to others as it has to himself.

AMHERST COLLEGE LIBRARY,
JUNE 10TH, 1876.

Those interested will find fuller explanations and remarks in the Library volume now being printed by the Bureau of Education at Washington.

INFORMATION,
PHILOSOPHY,
RELIGION,
GOVERNMENT,
ENGINEERING,
ART,
SOCIETY,
ECONOMICS,
HISTORY.

Table of Contents

0—Information

000—GENERAL WORKS

001. Intellectual life
002. History of the book
003. System theory
004. Computers
005. Computer programming
006. Cognitive science

006.6. Computer graphics

010—BIBLIOGRAPHY

011. General bibliographies
012. Bibliographies of individuals
014. Anonyms and pseudonyms
015. National bibliographies
016. Special bibliographies
017. Classified catalogs
017. Library catalogs
018. Author catalogs
019. Dictionary catalogs

020—LIBRARY SCIENCE

021. Management of libraries
022. Library architecture
023. Library employees
025. Library administration
026. Special libraries
026. Special collections
027. General libraries
028. Books and reading

030—ENCYCLOPEDIAS

031. American encyclopedias
032. British encyclopedias
033. German encyclopedias
034. French encyclopedias
035. Italian encyclopedias
036. Spanish encyclopedias
037. Slavic encyclopedias
038. Scandinavian encyclopedias
039. Other encyclopedias

050—PERIODICALS

051. American periodicals
052. English periodicals
053. German periodicals
054. French periodicals
055. Italian periodicals
056. Spanish periodicals
057. Slavic periodicals
058. Scandinavian periodicals
059. Periodicals of other languages

060—SOCIETIES

061. American societies
062. English societies
063. German societies
064. French societies
065. Italian societies
066. Spanish societies
067. Slavic societies
068. Other learned societies
069. Museums

070—JOURNALISM

071. American newspapers
072. English newspapers
073. German newspapers
074. French newspapers
075. Italian newspapers
076. Spanish newspapers
077. Slavic newspapers
078. Scandinavian newspapers
079. Other newspapers

080—ANTHOLOGIES

081. American anthologies
082. English anthologies
083. German anthologies
084. French anthologies
085. Italian anthologies
086. Spanish anthologies
087. Slavic anthologies
088. Scandinavian anthologies
089. Other anthologies

090—RARE BOOKS

091. Manuscripts and autographs
092. Block books
093. Early printed books
094. Privately printed books
095. Rare bindings
096. Rare illustrations or materials
097. Bookplates and ownership
098. Banned, lost, imaginary books
099. Other book rarities

1—Philosophy

100—PHILOSOPHY

101. Philosophy introductions
102. Philosophy outlines
103. Philosophy dictionaries
105. Philosophy periodicals
106. Philosophical societies
107. Philosophy study and teaching
108. Philosophy collections
109. Philosophy history

110—GENERAL METAPHYSICS

111. Ontology
113. Cosmology
114. Space (philosophical sense)
115. Time (philosophical sense)
116. Movement (philosophical)
117. Matter (philosophical sense)
118. Power (philosophical sense)
119. Mathematics (philosophical)

120—METAPHYSICAL TOPICS

121. Theory of knowledge
122. Cause and effect
123. Free will and determinism
124. Teleology
126. Self and consciousness
127. Unconsciousness
128. Soul and human beings
129. Immortality and future life

130—MIND AND BODY

131. Mental health
133. Occultism
135. Dreams
137. Personality and Temperament
138. Physiognomy
139. Phrenology

140—IDEOLOGY

141. Idealism
142. Criticism (philosophy)
143. Philosophical intuition
144. Empiricism and Humanism
145. Sensationalism
146. Materialism and Positivism
147. Pantheism and Monism
148. Eclecticism
149. Other philosophical systems

150—PSYCHOLOGY

152. Psychophysiology
153. Thought and thinking
154. Subconsciousness
155. Creativity and imagination

156. Comparative psychology
158. Sensibility and emotions

160—LOGIC

161. Induction (Logic)
162. Deductive logic
165. Fallacies (Logic) and Paradox
166. Syllogism and Enthymeme
167. Hypothesis
168. Argument and persuasion
169. Analogy

170—ETHICS

171. Theories of ethics
172. Political ethics
173. Family ethics
174. Professional ethics

> 174.1. *Clergy and professional ethics*
> 174.2. *Bioethics and medical ethics*
> 174.3. *Legal ethics*
> 174.4. *Business ethics*
> 174.6. *Gambling*
> 174.7. *Honor and honesty*
> 174.9. *Other professional ethical issues*

175. Ethics of amusements

176. Sexual ethics
177. Social ethics
178. Temperance and stimulants
179. Other ethical topics

180—ANCIENT PHILOSOPHY

181. Asian philosophy
182. Ancient Greek philosophy
183. Sophists and Socrates
184. Plato and Platonists
185. Aristotle and Peripatetics
186. Skeptics and Neoplatonism
187. Epicurus and Epicureans
188. Stoics
189. Medieval philosophy

190—MODERN PHILOSOPHY

191. American philosophy
192. British philosophy
193. German philosophy
194. French philosophy
195. Italian philosophy
196. Spanish philosophy
197. Russian and Slavic philosophy
198. Scandinavian philosophy
199. Other modern philosophers

2—Religion

200—RELIGION

201. Philosophy of religion
202. Religious systems
203. Religion encyclopedias
204. Religious essays
205. Religious periodicals
206. Religion societies
207. Religious education
208. Religion collections
209. History of religion

210—NATURAL THEOLOGY

211. Deism and Atheism
212. Pantheism and Theosophy
213. Creation and Evolution
214. Providence and Theodicy
215. Religion and science
218. Eternity (Christian)

220—BIBLE

221. Old Testament
222. Historical Books (O.T.)

223. Poetical books (O.T.)
224. Prophetic books (O.T.)
225. New Testament
226. Gospels and Acts (N.T.)
227. Epistles (N.T.)
228. Revelation (N.T.)
229. Apocryphal books

230—DOCTRINAL THEOLOGY

231. God
232. Jesus Christ
233. Theological anthropology
234. Salvation
235. Angels, demons, and saints
236. Eschatology
238. Creeds and Catechisms
239. Apologetics

240—DEVOTIONAL LITERATURE

241. Christian ethics
242. Meditation and contemplation
243. Conversion and evangelism
246. Christian art and symbolism
247. Religious articles
248. Christian life
249. Families and religious life

250—PASTORAL THEOLOGY

251. Preaching
252. Sermons
253. Evangelistic work and Clergy
254. Church management
259. Other ministries

260—CHURCH

261. Church and the world
262. Church polity

263. Sabbath and church year
264. Public worship
265. Sacraments
266. Missions and home missions
267. Christian associations`
268. Christian education
269. Revivals and Spiritual retreats

270—CHURCH HISTORY

271. Monasticism
272. Persecution
273. Christian heresies
274. European Christianity
275. Asian Christianity
276. African Christianity
277. North American Christianity
278. South American Christianity
279. Oceanian Christianity

280—CHRISTIAN SECTS

281. Early church history
282. Catholic Church
283. Anglican Communion
284. Protestant churches
285. Reformed churches
286. Baptists
287. Methodism
289. Other Christian sects

290—RELIGIONS

291. Mythology
292. Classical mythology
293. Germanic mythology
294. Hinduism and Buddhism
295. Zoroastrianism
296. Judaism
297. Islam and Bahai Faith
299. Other religions

3—Government

300—GOVERNMENT

301. Legislative bodies
304. Law

304.1. International law
304.2. Constitutional law
304.3. Criminal law
304.4. Martial law
304.5. United States law
304.6. Great Britain law
304.7. Common law
304.8. Canon law
304.9. Law in other jurisdictions

305. Public administration

305.1. Public administration
305.2. Local government
305.3. United States government
305.4. Non-US governments
305.5. Military art and science
305.56. Infantry
305.57. Cavalry
305.59. Naval art and science

306. Home economics

306.6 Household employees
306.7. Child rearing and parenting

307. Education

307.2. Teaching and School management
307.3. Elementary and Kindergarten
307.4. Secondary and High schools
307.5. Adult and Continuing education
307.6. Education Curricula
307.8. Universities and colleges
307.9. State and Public schools

310—SCIENCE

311. Philosophy of science

312. Science outlines
313. Science encyclopedias
315. Science periodicals
316. Science societies
317. Scientific research
318. Collections of scientific essays
319. Science history

320—MATHEMATICS

321. Arithmetic
322. Algebra
323. Geometry
324. Trigonometry and topology
325. Calculus and math analysis
326. Algebraic geometry
328. Numerical analysis
329. Probability and statistics

330—ASTRONOMY

331. Theoretical astronomy
332. Spherical astronomy
333. Descriptive astronomy
335. Earth
336. Geodesy
337. Navigation
338. Ephemerides
339. Chronology

340—PHYSICS

341. Mechanics
342. Fluid mechanics
343. Gas dynamics
344. Sound
345. Optics and Light
346. Heat and Thermodynamics
347. Electricity
348. Magnetism
349. Nuclear physics and Matter

350—CHEMISTRY

351. Physical, theoretical chemistry
352. Chemical laboratories
353. Analytic chemistry
356. Inorganic chemistry
357. Organic chemistry
358. Crystallography
359. Mineralogy

360—GEOLOGY

361. Physical geology

361.5. Rocks and minerals

362. Economic geology
364. Geology of Europe
365. Geology of Asia
366. Geology of Africa
367. Geology of North America
368. Geology of South America
369. Oceania, polar, other regions

369.4. Geology of Australia
369.9. Astrogeology

370—PALEONTOLOGY

371. Paleobotany
372. Invertebrate fossil
373. Protozoa fossils
374. Mollusk fossils
375. Arthropoda fossils
376. Vertebrates fossils
377. Fish, amphibian, reptile fossils

377.9. Dinosaurs

378. Bird fossils
379. Mammal fossils

380—BIOLOGY

381. Prehistoric peoples
382. Anthropology
383. Physical anthropology
385. Evolution and genetics
386. Microbiology
387. Life (Biology)
388. Microscopy
389. Biological specimens

390—PHYSIOLOGY

391. Plant physiology and anatomy
392. Phanerogams and trees
393. Dicotyledons
394. Monocotyledons
395. Gymnosperms
396. Cryptogams
397. Pteridophyta
398. Bryophytes
399. Zoology

399.1 Animal physiology
399.2. Invertebrates
399.3. Protozoa
399.4. Mollusks
399.5. Arthropoda and worms
399.6. Vertebrates
399.7. Fishes, amphibians and reptiles
399.8. Birds
399.9. Mammals

4—Engineering

400—APPLIED SCIENCES

401. Philosophy of technology
402. Formulas, recipes, etc.
403. Technology dictionaries
404. Technology essays
405. Technology periodicals
406. Technology societies
407. Technical education
408. Inventions and Patents

409. History of technology

410—MEDICINE

411. Anatomy
412. Physiology

412.1. Cardiovascular system
412.2. Respiration
412.3. Digestion
412.4. Glands
412.5. Animal heat
412.6. Reproduction
412.7. Musculoskeletal, Larynx, Skin
412.8. Nervous system
412.81. Nerves, Peripheral
412.82. Central nervous system and Brain
412.84. Vision
412.85. Hearing
412.86. Smell
412.87. Taste
412.88. Touch
412.9. Other parts of the body

413. Health and Hygiene
414. Public health
415. Drugs and pharmacy

415.8. Physical medicine
415.84. Medical radiology
415.85. Mental healing
415.88. Patent medicines
415.88. Traditional medicine
415.892. Acupuncture

416. Diseases and Treatment
417. Surgery and Dentistry
418. Gynecology and Pediatrics

420—AGRICULTURE

421. Farms, soils, and plants
422. Agricultural hindrances
423. Field crops
424. Tree crops, fruit, and nuts
425. Gardening (for food)
426. Domestic animals and Pets
427. Dairying
428. Bee culture and Sericulture
429. Hunting and Fishing (for food)

440—ENGINEERING

441. Mechanical engineering

441.1. Steam engineering
421.2. Hydraulic machinery
421.3. Electrical engineering
421.4. Heat engineering
421.5. Pneumatics and refrigeration
421.6. Fans and pumping machinery
421.7. Production engineering
421.8. Other machinery topics
421.9. Machine-tools

442. Mining engineering
443. Military engineering

443.8. Weapons and Armor (regimental)

444. Civil engineering
445. Railroads and roads
447. Hydraulic engineering
448. Sanitary engineering
449. Other branches of engineering

450—CHEMICAL ENGINEERING

451. Chemicals
452. Explosives and Fuel
453. Beverages
454. Food
455. Petroleum, Oils, and fats
456. Ceramics, Clay, and Cement
457. Pigments, Paint, and printing
458. Polymers and Plastics
459. Metallurgy and Assaying

460—MANUFACTURING

461. Metal-work
462. Ironwork and Steelwork
463. Brass and Bronze
464. Forest products
465. Leather
466. Paper and Paper products
467. Textile fabrics
468. Rubber
469. Other manufactured goods

480—HANDICRAFT

481. Scientific apparatus
482. Blacksmithing
483. Firearms and Locksmithing
484. Woodwork and Furniture
485. Footwear and Leather industry

486. Bookbinding and Printing
487. Clothing trade

487.6. Clothing, fashion, and beauty

488. Toys, jewelry, and packaging
489. Basket making

490—BUILDING

491. Building materials
492. Architecture design

492.3. Dwellings

493. Masonry and build techniques
494. Carpentry
495. Roofing
496. Plumbing and Pipe fitting

496.8. Household sanitation

497. Heating and Ventilation
498. Painting and Paperhanging
499. Railroad cars

5—Art

500—ARTS

501. Philosophy of art
502. Art surveys and introductions
503. Art encyclopedias
504. Essays in the arts
505. Art periodicals
506. Art societies
507. Art study and teaching
508. Art museums
509. Art history

510—GARDENING

511. City planning
512. Gardens
513. Scenic byways
514. Water in landscaping
515. Shrubs and ornamental trees
516. Gardening (ornamental)
517. Garden decor and furniture
518. Sepulchral monuments
519. Cemeteries

520—ARCHITECTURE

521. Architectural design
522. Ancient architecture
523. Medieval architecture
524. Modern architecture

525. Public architecture
526. Religious architecture
527. Educational architecture
528. Domestic architecture

528.5. House furnishings

529. Decoration and ornament

530—SCULPTURE

531. Sculpture technique
532. Ancient sculpture
533. Classical sculpture
534. Medieval sculpture
535. Modern sculpture
536. Carving, Gems, and Glyptics
537. Coins and medals
538. Pottery
539. Art metal-work

540—DRAWING AND DESIGN

541. Drawing technique
542. Perspective
543. Artistic anatomy
544. Mechanical drawing
545. Decorative arts
546. Needlework and Fancy work
547. Interior decoration
548. Glassware and Glass art

549. Artistic furniture

550—PAINTING

551. Painting technique
552. Color in art
553. Epic and mythic painting
554. Genre painting
555. Religious art
556. Historical painting
557. Portraits
558. Landscape painting
559. Painting of specific regions

560—ENGRAVING

561. Engraving and relief printing
562. Cooper and steel engraving
563. Lithography
564. Chromolitho- and serigraphy
565. Line and stipple engraving
566. Mezzotint and Aquatint
567. Etchers and Etching
568. Machine engraving
569. Printers and Engravers

570—PHOTOGRAPHY

571. Photography technique
572. Color photography
573. Photography oil processes

574. Holography
575. Digital photography
576. Digital art
577. Photoengraving
578. Photographic applications
579. Photographers

580—MUSIC

581. Music theory
582. Dramatic music
583. Sacred music
584. Vocal and popular music
585. Orchestral music
586. Keyboard instruments
587. Stringed instruments
588. Wind instruments

590—RECREATION

591. Public entertainment
592. Theater
593. Indoor amusements
594. Games of skill
595. Games of chance
596. Sports and Athletics
597. Boats and aeronautical sports
598. Horsemanship and Dog sports
599. Hunting, fishing, and shooting

599.9. Weapons and Armor (personal)

6—Society

600—SOCIAL SCIENCES

601. Sociology
602. Social psychology
603. Social science encyclopedias
604. Social science essays

604.2. Human ecology
604.5. Sociobiology
604.6. Population

604.8. Migrations

605. Social science periodicals
606. Culture
607. Social science research

607.9. Statistics
607.94. Europe statistics
607.95. Asia statistics
607.96. Africa statistics
607.97. North America statistics

607.98. *South America statistics*
607.99. *Oceania and Polar statistics*

608. Political science

608.1. *Political science philosophy*
608.2. *Religion and state*
608.3. *Human rights and Minorities*
608.4. *Elections and Suffrage*
608.5. *Colonies and Emigration*
608.6. *Slavery and African Americans*
608.7. *International relations*

609. Ethnology

609.1. *Costume and Cosmetics*
609.2. *Families and Courtship*
609.3. *Death and Funeral rites*
609.4. *Manners and customs*
609.5. *Etiquette*
609.52. *Entertaining*
609.58. *Cooking and Gastronomy*

610—LANGUAGE

611. Language philosophy
612. Language outlines
613. Language dictionaries
614. Language essays
615. Language periodicals
616. Language societies
617. Language study
618. Linguistics collections
619. Historical linguistics

619.1. *Linguistics*
619.11. *Writing and alphabet*
619.12. *Semantics and etymology*
619.13. *Lexicography*
619.14. *Phonology and Phonetics*
619.15. *Grammar*
619.17. *Paleography and Inscriptions*
619.18. *Language acquisition*
619.19. *Sign language*

620—ENGLISH LANGUAGE

621. English language Phonetics
622. English language Semantics
623. English language Lexicography
625. English language Grammar
627. English language Dialects
628. English language Usage

629. Old English

630—GERMAN LANGUAGE

631. German language Phonetics
632. German language Etymology
633. German Lexicography
635. German language Grammar
637. German language Dialects
638. German language Usage
639. Other Germanic languages

640—FRENCH LANGUAGE

641. French language Phonetics
642. French language Semantics
643. French language Lexicography
645. French language Grammar
647. French language Dialects
648. French language Usage
649. Catalan and Provençal

650—ITALIAN LANGUAGE

651. Italian language Phonetics
652. Italian language Semantics
653. Italian language Lexicography
655. Italian language Grammar
657. Italian language Dialects
658. Italian language Usage
659. Romanian language

660—SPANISH LANGUAGE

661. Spanish language Phonetics
662. Spanish language Semantics
663. Spanish Lexicography
665. Spanish language Grammar
667. Spanish language Dialects
668. Spanish language Usage
669. Portuguese language

670—LATIN LANGUAGE

671. Latin language Pronunciation
672. Latin language Semantics
673. Latin language Dictionaries
675. Latin language Grammar
677. Latin language Dialects
678. Latin language Usage
679. Romance languages

680—GREEK LANGUAGE

681. Greek language Alphabet
682. Greek language Semantics
683. Greek language Lexicography
685. Greek language Grammar
687. Greek language Dialects
688. Greek language study
689. Modern Greek language

690—OTHER LANGUAGES

691. Indo-European languages
692. Semitic languages
693. Hamitic languages
694. Altaic and Uralic languages
695. East Asian languages
696. African languages
697. North American Indian languages
698. South American Indian languages
699. Austronesian, other languages

7—Economics

730—ECONOMICS

731. Labor and Capital
732. Finance
733. Land use
734. Cooperation
735. Socialism and Communism
736. Finance, Public
737. International economics
738. Industries and Prices
739. Macroeconomics and poor

760—SOCIAL SERVICE

761. Charity
762. Hospitals and Asylums

762.1. Hospitals
762.2. Mentally ill
762.3. People with mental disabilities
762.4. Disabled, Blind, and Deaf
762.5. Poor (social service perspectives)
762.6. Older people care
762.7. Child welfare
762.8. Other human services
762.9. Social service in particular areas

763. Political activists

763.1. Risk and Accidents
763.2. Police
763.31. Censorship

763.32. Terrorism
763.33. Gun control
763.34. Disasters
763.35. Civil defense
763.37. Fire departments
763.41. Prohibition (political movement)
763.42. Gambling law and legislation
763.45. Drug control
763.46. Abortion government policy
763.47. Pornography
763.5. Housing
763.6. Public utilities
763.7. Environmental protection
763.728. Refuse and refuse disposal
763.73. Pollution
763.7386 Acid rain
763.8. Food supply
763.9. Birth control and Overpopulation

764. Criminology
765. Correctional institutions
766. Secret societies
767. Clubs
768. Insurance
769. Other associations

770—BUSINESS

771. Office management
772. Business communication
773. Shorthand and Dictation

777. Accounting and Bookkeeping
778. Management
779. Publicity and Marketing

780—COMMERCE

781. Commerce
782. International trade
783. Postal service
784. Telecommunication

784.1. Telegraph

784.3. Internet
784.4. Cables, Submarine
784.5. Broadcasting
784.6. Telephone
784.8. Motion picture industry

785. Railroads (usage perspectives)
786. Waterways
787. Shipping
788. Local transit
789. Weights, measures, Metrology

8—History

800—LITERATURE

800.1. Philosophy of Literature
800.2. Literary compendia and outlines
800.3. Literature Dictionaries
800.4. Literature Periodicals
800.5. Literature Societies, etc.
800.6. Literature study
800.7. Rhetoric and Style, Literary
800.8. Specific topics in literature
800.9. Folklore

801. American literature

801.1. American poetry
801.2. American drama
801.3. American fiction
801.4. American essays
801.5. American Speeches
801.6. American letters
801.7. American wit and humor
801.8. American authors and miscellany

802. English literature

802.1. English poetry
802.2. English drama
802.3. English fiction
802.4. English essays
802.5. English speeches
802.6. English letters
802.7. English wit and humor

802.8. English authors and miscellany
802.9. Old English literature

803. German literature

803.1. German poetry
803.2. German drama
803.3. German fiction
803.4. German essays
803.5. German speeches
803.6. German letters
803.7. German wit and humor
803.8. German authors and miscellany
803.9. Other Germanic literature

804. French literature

804.1. French poetry
804.2. French drama
804.3. French fiction
804.4. French essays
804.5. French speeches
804.6. French letters
804.7. French wit and humor
804.8. French authors and miscellany
804.9. Provençal and Catalan literature

805. Italian literature

805.1. Italian poetry
805.2. Italian drama
805.3. Italian fiction
805.4. Italian essays

805.5. *Italian speeches, addresses, etc.*
805.5. *Spanish speeches, addresses, etc.*
805.6. *Italian letters*
805.7. *Italian wit and humor*
805.7. *Spanish wit and humor*
805.8. *Italian authors and miscellany*
805.9. *Romanian literature*

806. Spanish literature

806.1. *Spanish poetry*
806.2. *Spanish drama*
806.3. *Spanish fiction*
806.4. *Spanish essays*
806.6. *Spanish letters*
806.8. *Spanish authors and miscellany*
806.9. *Portuguese literature*

807. Latin literature

807.1. *Latin poetry*
807.2. *Latin drama*
807.3. *Epic poetry, Latin*
807.4. *Latin lyric poetry*
807.5. *Speeches, addresses, etc., Latin.*
807.6. *Latin letters*
807.7. *Latin wit and humor*
807.8. *Latin authors and miscellany*
807.9. *Latin literature*

808. Greek and classical literature

808.1. *Greek poetry and Classical poetry*
808.2. *Greek and classical drama*
808.3. *Epic poetry*
808.4. *Greek and classical lyric poetry*
808.5. *Greek speeches, addresses, etc.*
808.6. *Greek and classical letters*
808.7. *Greek wit and humor*
808.8. *Greek authors and miscellany*
808.9. *Modern Greek literature*

809. Literature of other languages

809.1. *Other Indo-European literature*
809.2. *Semitic literature*
809.3. *Literature of Hamitic languages*
809.4. *Altaic and Uralic literature*
809.5. *East Asian literature*
809.6. *African literature*
809.7. *North American Indian literature*
809.8. *South American Indian literature*
809.9. *Austronesian literature*

810—HISTORY AND PLACES

811. Philosophy of history
812. Historical chronology
813. History encyclopedias
814. Historical essays
815. History periodicals
816. History societies
817. History study and teaching
818. Historical collections
819. Modern histories

820—GEOGRAPHY

821. Historical geography
822. Maps and Atlases
823. Antiquities and Archaeology
824. Europe description and travel
825. Asia description and travel
826. Africa description and travel
827. America description and travel

827.5. *Latin, South America travel*

828. Oceania, polar region travel

830—ANCIENT HISTORY

831. Ancient China
832. Ancient Egypt
833. Ancient Judea
834. Ancient India
835. History of Iraq and Iran
836. Europe history
837. Ancient Rome
838. Ancient Greece
839. Ancient history in other areas

840—EUROPE

841. Scotland and Ireland
842. England and Great Britain
843. Germany and Central Europe
844. France
845. Italy
846. Spain and Portugal
847. Russia, Finland, East Europe
848. Scandinavia
849. Smaller European countries

849.1. *Iceland*
849.2. *Netherlands*

849.3. *Belgium*
849.4. *Switzerland*
849.5. *Greece and Byzantine Empire*
849.6. *Turkey and Balkan Peninsula*
849.7. *Bulgaria and Former Yugoslavia*
849.8. *Romania*
849.9. *Aegean Islands and Crete*

850—ASIA

851. China and Korea
852. Japan
853. Arabian Peninsula
854. India, Pakistan, and Bangladesh
855. Iran
856. Middle East
857. Siberia (Russia)
857. Asia, Central
858. Afghanistan
859. Southeast Asia

860—AFRICA

861. North Africa

861.1. *Tunisia*
861.2. *Libya*

862. Egypt and Sudan

862.4. *Sudan*

863. Ethiopia and Eritrea

863.5. *Eritrea*

864. Morocco and Western Sahara

864.8. *Western Sahara*

865. Algeria
866. West Africa
867. Sub-Saharan Africa
868. South Africa
869. Madagascar and Indian Ocean

870—NORTH AMERICA

871. Canada

871.1. *British Columbia*
871.2. *Northwest, Canadian*
871.23 *Alberta*
871.24 *Saskatchewan*
871.27 *Manitoba*

871.3. *Ontario*
871.4. *Québec (Province)*
871.5. *New Brunswick and Atlantic*
871.6. *Nova Scotia and Acadia*
871.7. *Prince Edward Island*
871.8. *Newfoundland and Labrador*
871.9. *Canada, Northern*

872. Mexico and Central America
873. United States
874. New England

874.1. *Maine*
874.2. *New Hampshire*
874.3. *Vermont*
874.4. *Massachusetts*
874.5. *Rhode Island*
874.6. *Connecticut*
874.7. *New York (State)*
874.8. *Pennsylvania*
874.9. *New Jersey*

875. South, Gulf, Old Southwest

875.1. *Delaware*
875.2. *Maryland*
875.3. *Washington (D.C.)*
875.4. *West Virginia*
875.5. *Virginia*
875.6. *North Carolina*
875.7. *South Carolina*
875.8. *Georgia*
875.9. *Florida*
876.1. *Alabama*
876.2. *Mississippi*
876.3. *Louisiana*
876.4. *Texas*
876.6. *Oklahoma*
876.7. *Arkansas*
876.8. *Tennessee*
876.9. *Kentucky*

877. Middle West

877.1. *Ohio*
877.2. *Indiana*
877.3. *Illinois*
877.4. *Michigan*
877.5. *Wisconsin*
877.6. *Minnesota*
877.7. *Iowa*
877.8. *Missouri*

878. Great plains, mountain west

878.1. *Kansas*
878.2. *Nebraska*
878.3. *South Dakota*
878.4. *North Dakota*
878.6. *Montana*
878.7. *Wyoming*
878.8. *Colorado*
878.9. *New Mexico*

879. Far western states

879.1. *Arizona*
879.2. *Utah*
879.3. *Nevada*
879.4. *California*
879.5. *Oregon*
879.6. *Idaho*
879.7. *Washington (State)*
879.8. *Alaska*

880—SOUTH AMERICA

881. Brazil
882. Argentina
883. Chile
884. Bolivia
885. Peru
886. Panama, Colombia, Ecuador
887. Venezuela
888. Suriname and Guyana
889. Paraguay and Uruguay

890—OCEANIA AND POLAR

891. Indonesia and Philippines

891.1. *Borneo*
891.2. *Celebes (Indonesia)*
891.3. *Maluku (Indonesia)*
891.4. *Philippines*
892.1. *Sumatra (Indonesia)*
892.2. *Java (Indonesia)*

893. Australasia

893.1. *New Zealand*
893.2. *New Caledonia*
893.3. *Loyalty Islands (New Caledonia)*
893.4. *Vanuatu*
893.5. *Solomon Islands*
893.6. *New Britain and Ireland Island*
893.7. *Admiralty Islands*

894. Australia
895. New Guinea
896. Polynesia

896.1. *Fiji, Tonga, and Samoan Islands*
896.2. *Society, Austral, and Cook*
896.3. *Marquesas and Tuamotu*
896.4. *Kiritimati and Minor Polynesia*
896.5. *Micronesia*
896.6. *Caroline Islands and Palau*
896.7. *Mariana Islands and Guam*
896.8. *Marshall Islands and Kiribati*
896.9. *Hawaii*

897. Isolated islands
898. Polar regions

898.8. *Antarctica*
898.9. *Outer space*

899. Biography

Subject Index

When creating a card catalog, subjects are to be put in an Alphabetical INDEX. The number following it is its Class Number. The entire resources of the library on this subject will be found under this number either in the Subject Catalogue, the Shelf Catalogue, or on the shelves.

Where a class number ends in a cipher, the subject will be found, on reference to the prefixed classification, to be subdivided.

EXPLANATIONS

The titles of the subject catalogue are exact transcriptions of the title page, neither amended, translated, or in any way altered, except that mottoes, titles of authors, repetitions, or matter of any kind not essential to a clear titular description, are *omitted*. Omissions of mottoes are indicated by three stars (* * *); of other matter by three dots (..). The phraseology, spelling, and punctuation of the title are exactly copied; but capitals are given only to proper names and adjectives, and initial words of sentences. Any additions needed to make the title clear are supplied and enclosed by brackets.

After the titles, are given in order: the place of publication; the year; the year of copyright, if different, in brackets; the edition; the number of volumes, or of pages if in only one volume; the illustrations, maps, plates, or portraits; and the size nearest in the arbitrary scale, regardless of the fold of the sheet. This scale gives the heights in decimeters. Square and oblong books have the size prefixed by *sq.* or *ob.* Books 1 decimeter high are called 32°; 1.5 deci., 16°; 2 deci., 12°; 2.5 deci., 8°; 3 deci., 4°; and all others are marked simply by the nearest height, i.e. a book marked 4 is between 3.5 and 4.5 decimeters high. In books having more than one pagination the number of pages is indicated by giving the last number of each pagination connected by a +; an added + indicates additional matter unpaged.

These imprint entries give the facts regardless of the title page, and are left blank only when they can be ascertained neither from the book itself or other sources.

The contents of volumes are given when on title pages, or when necessary to properly identify the volume, but no analysis is attempted. Necessary notes are given at the bottom of the subject card after the imprint entries.

Duplicates are simply marked copy 2, copy 3, etc., and bear the same class and book number, but editions of the same book distinct in character are catalogued separately.

In all the catalogues, books are entered under the *surnames* of authors when known; under the *initials* of author's names, when these only appear, the last initial being put first; under the *pseudonyms* of the writers, when the real names are not ascertained; under the names of *editors* of collections; under the names of *countries, cities, societies,* or other *bodies* which are responsible for their publication; under the *first word* not an article of the titles of periodicals and of anonymous books the names of whose authors are not ascertained. *Commentaries* with the text, and *translations* are entered under the heading of the original work, but commentaries without the text are entered under the name of the *commentator.* The Bible or any part of it in any language is entered under the word *Bible.* Books having more than one author are entered under the first named on the title.

In the headings of titles, the names of authors are given in their vernacular form. In English and French surnames beginning with a prefix (except the French de and d') the name is recorded under the prefix. In other languages and in French names beginning with de and d', the name is recorded under the word following the prefix. Compound surnames are entered under the first part of the name. Noblemen and ecclesiastical dignitaries are entered under their family names, but *sovereigns, princes, oriental writers, friars, persons canonized,* and all other persons known *only* by their first name, are entered under this first name.

The catalogue is not a biographical dictionary, so only gives the names of authors with sufficient fullness to distinguish them from each other in practical use.

Names in FULL FACE TYPE are the ruling headings under which the books are entered in the various catalogues. Entries not beginning with this type are in addition to the first or main entry, and are made under the names of *translators, editors, commentators, continuators,* etc., as participators in the authorship; also in the case of books having more than one author, or having both generic and specific titles, or published by societies or other bodies, and having also the name of the individual author. These additional entries are made in order to carry out the plan of the Authors' Catalogue, which aims to give under each author's name all his works which the library contains.

The works of an author known by more than one name are given all together, under the form of name chosen. Any other name or title by which he may be known, if it differs in the first three letters, is entered in its alphabetical place, followed by the word *see* and the name under which the books are entered. Such cross references have no titles given under them, but are simply guides to the name chosen.

A single dash indicates the omission of the preceding heading; a subsequent dash indicates the omission of a subordinate heading or of a title. A dash connecting numbers signifies *to and including*; following a number it signifies *continuation*. A ? following a word or entry signifies *probably*. Brackets enclose words added to titles or changed in form.

The German diphthongs ä, ö, ü are written, ae, oe, ue.

Dates are all given in years of the common calendar, and Arabic numerals are uniformly used for all numbers.

Subject Catalogue

The Subject Catalogue on large cards can be used to advantage only with the aid of the *Classification* or *Index*. To find what the library has on any given subject, get from the Index the class number of that subject. Under this number in the Subject Catalogue will be found the full titles of the books, with imprints, cross references, and notes. The class number, by which the cards are arranged, is given in the upper left corner and immediately under it is the book number. Any other class number given in the left hand margin refers to another subject of which the book also treats. When the class number at the top is followed by an additional figure in brackets, the subject as given in the printed scheme has been subdivided in arranging the cards. This subdivision will be found on the first card of the catalogue which bears this class number. These figures in brackets determine the arrangement of the titles in the Catalogue, but on the shelves, in the Shelf Catalogue, and in calling for and charging books, they are entirely disregarded. Thus a book numbered 942(7).14 would be in the Catalogue among the 942 cards arranged by the figure in brackets as though it were a decimal, but it would be called for as 942.14, the brackets indicating that the final classing was limited to the Catalogue and was not extended to the shelves. If a fourth figure is added without brackets, the final classing is extended to the shelves as well as to the catalogue, and all the figures must be used in calling for the book. In such cases the added figure is treated as a decimal in the arrangement, though the decimal point is not written.

The last card which bears any class number, gives under that number, followed by the word See the call numbers of other books which treat of the same subject, but are classed elsewhere. General cross references are also made in many cases without specifying individual books, as from *Commerce* as a question of Economics (740) to *Commerce* as Engineering, Book-keeping Business Manuals, etc. (450). In such cases there is a card under 740 marked See 450, and under 450 there is a card marked See 740. From whatever standpoint a subject is approached, the cross references guide at once to the same subject treated in its other relations. These cross references both general and specific are often accompanied by brief notes, characterizing the books to which reference is made.

There will be found at the beginning of many class numbers, a card noting the most reliable books on that subject, and the best of the articles in periodicals, transactions, and collected works with the volume and page where they may be found. It is hoped to give special prominence to these notes for the guidance of readers, and they will be added as rapidly as other duties allow.

Many subjects will have no sub-section cards at the beginning; some will have no reference cards at the end; and some may have no titles given under the number. The scheme provides a place for books on all subjects, whether the library has them or not, so where no titles are given under a class number it shows that the library has as yet no books on that subject.

Articles in periodicals and transactions, separate volumes of sets and collections which are located together, *if catalogued* are put under their proper subject number, but no *book number* is given with it. The call number of the book, where they may be found, is always given in the margin preceded by the word IN. In the same way special chapters in books will sometimes be catalogued, *e.g.* a card marked 338 IN 331-27, would mean that in the 27 books on 331, *Capital and Labor*, there was a chapter on 338, *Production*.

DIGITAL ORGANIZATION

Dewey's system allows us to use an intuitive, general-to-specific ordering of content and labels based on numbers instead of words to organize a large number of items. This can apply not just to hardcopy books but to all media types including digital materials.

When organizing digital files, consider the following tips: (1) enumerate files using the aforementioned system; (2) keep up with technologies and make sure whatever approach is selected is universal, durable, usable, and timeless enough to survive future storage formats—upgrade when necessary; (3) group items when possible—such as using folders to organize large numbers of files—but don't group so much it becomes difficult to find files; (4) use the shortest, clearest names possible; (5) minimize use of special characters, spaces, and punctuation; (6) distinguish words with capitalization not punctuation or spacing; (7) consider naming with start and stop dates, version numbers, author initials, project names, categories, media types, and/or unique identification numbers for clarity, and (8) sequence components of a name from general to specific: if the file is a song then name it *"Song<NameOfSong>"*, if named after a person name it *"<LastNameOfPerson> <FirstName>"*, etc.

Naming is more an art than a science. Try to find a nice balance of the above criteria. Consider the possibilities and select a naming convention most beneficial to your collection. For example, possible names for a project folder could be:

2015.120.Project.TheClassificationOfEverything
2015.120.ClassificationOfEverything
2015.ClassificationOfE
2015.COE
COE

and possible names for a file could be:

150228.120.Book.TheClassificationOfEverything.v1_43.jmo.txt
150228.Book.ClassificationOfE.1_43.txt
150228.COE-1aq.txt
coe-1aq.txt

Longer names communicate more details to the user. For small collections, long names should not be necessary. However, the larger a collection gets the longer item names need to be for clarity easier identification in a list. Likewise, the larger a library, the more time, effort, and consideration will be required for its planning, organization, and maintenance.